THE WITCHES

In England in the 1600s many people believed in witches. A witch could be an old woman, or a young woman – sometimes even a man or a boy. But they were usually women, and everybody was very afraid of them. Because a witch could kill you – just with a curse.

In 1612, near Pendle Hill in Lancashire, lived a girl called Jennet Device. She was nine years old then, poor, thin, and hungry. She had no shoes, no coat, and sometimes nothing to eat for days. Life was not easy for Jennet Device.

And her grandmother, Old Demdike, was a witch. Her mother Elizabeth was a witch, and her sister Alizon. Even her poor stupid brother James was a witch . . . Or that is what the villagers believed.

This is Jennet's story of her family. It begins in 1634, when Jennet is a prisoner in Lancaster Castle . . .

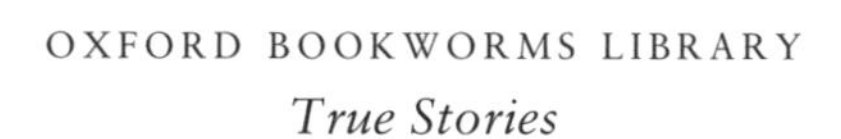

OXFORD BOOKWORMS LIBRARY

True Stories

The Witches of Pendle

Stage 1 (400 headwords)

Series Editor: Jennifer Bassett
Founder Editor: Tricia Hedge
Activities Editors: Jennifer Bassett and Alison Baxter

ROWENA AKINYEMI

The Witches of Pendle

OXFORD UNIVERSITY PRESS

OXFORD
UNIVERSITY PRESS

Great Clarendon Street, Oxford OX2 6DP

Oxford University Press is a department of the University of Oxford.
It furthers the University's objective of excellence in research, scholarship,
and education by publishing worldwide in

Oxford New York

Auckland Cape Town Dar es Salaam Hong Kong Karachi
Kuala Lumpur Madrid Melbourne Mexico City Nairobi
New Delhi Shanghai Taipei Toronto

With offices in

Argentina Austria Brazil Chile Czech Republic France Greece
Guatemala Hungary Italy Japan Poland Portugal Singapore
South Korea Switzerland Thailand Turkey Ukraine Vietnam

OXFORD and OXFORD ENGLISH are registered trade marks of
Oxford University Press in the UK and in certain other countries

First published in Oxford Bookworms 1994

11

ISBN 978 0 19 478924 0

A complete recording of this Bookworms edition of
The Witches of Pendle is available in an audio pack ISBN 978 0 19 478892 2

Typeset by Wyvern Typesetting Ltd, Bristol

Printed in China

Illustrated by: Susie Foster

Word count (main text): 5730 words

For more information on the Oxford Bookworms Library,
visit www.oup.com/elt/gradedreaders

CONTENTS

1
THE PEDLAR

The spring of 1634 arrives, but in the prison of Lancaster Castle it stays cold. The twenty women in the prison are dirty, hungry and cold. There are no beds or chairs and so they sleep on the cold floor. There are no windows, so it is always dark. The women want to get out of the prison; they want to go home. Sometimes the guards open the big, old door and put some bread and water on the floor. Then they close the door again.

My name is Jennet Device, and I am one of the twenty women in prison. Day after day, I sit on the cold floor and wait. I want to feel warm again; I want to see the sky again, and Pendle Hill, the beautiful hill near my home. But I am in the dark prison of Lancaster Castle, and I sit on the cold floor and wait.

One day, something happens. The guards open the big, old door. 'Jennet Device!' a guard calls. 'Come here at once, witch! Somebody wants to see you.'

I get up slowly because I'm very cold and I walk across the dark room to the door. Perhaps it's someone from Read Hall! Perhaps I'm going home!

'Jennet Device, be quick!' the guard calls again.

Someone is standing at the door with the guard. 'Jennet,' he says quietly.

Day after day, I sit on the cold floor and wait.

I see him then: a tall man with brown hair and tired blue eyes. He is not from Read Hall. It is Mr Webster, from the church at Kildwick. My legs stop moving and suddenly I want to sit down.

'Come on, come on,' the guard says angrily. He begins to close the door.

'Come out here for a minute, Jennet,' Mr Webster says quietly. 'Sit down and eat something.'

I sit down at a little table near the door. Mr Webster gives me some bread and some meat and I begin to eat hungrily.

'Ten minutes,' the guard says. 'After ten minutes, she goes in again.'

'Thank you,' Mr Webster says.

'How is everyone at Read Hall?' I ask at last.

Mr Webster smiles. 'Everyone is well. I was there yesterday.'

I close my eyes for a minute. 'Mr Webster, it's not true. I'm not a witch, you know.'

'I know, Jennet,' Mr Webster says. 'Last week, I brought Edmund Robinson and his father into my church, and asked them about the boy's story. Many people believed Edmund's story, but some people didn't. Edmund Robinson is going to London tomorrow with his father, and a judge is going to question them.'

The guard comes back and begins to open the door.

'Time!' he says.

Mr Webster stands up. 'God is here with you, Jennet. Never forget that. You can be happy, when God is with you.'

I stand up too, and take the bread from the table. 'Yes, Mr Webster. God is with me; I believe that.' But happy? How can I be happy?

I go back into the dark prison, and the guard closes the door behind me. The women run to me. 'Bread! Give us bread!' they cry.

Quickly, I put the bread in my shirt. I don't want to lose it. I walk across the room and sit down on the floor. I am crying, but I feel a little better. Edmund Robinson, of Newchurch, is only ten years old. Edmund told lies about me and about many women: he saw us at a witches' meeting at a house called Hoarstones. It's not true, but many people believed him. What is he going to say in London? The truth? Or more lies.

But now, in the prison of Lancaster Castle, I want to tell my story. It is a story about rich men and angry villagers; about old women and hungry children. It is a true story, and it happened to me.

I was born in 1603. My family was always very poor, and after my father died, we were poorer. In winter, I was often ill and I was always cold and hungry. In summer, I was sometimes ill and I was often cold and hungry. We lived some miles from the village of Newchurch, in an old house called Malkin Tower. It was dirty and cold. The rain came in through the windows and there were no doors. To the west, was the big hill called Pendle. Pendle Hill was beautiful. I loved Pendle Hill because it sat quietly all year and watched me.

Malkin Tower was dirty and cold.

My story begins on the eighteenth day of March in the year 1612. I was nine years old, and my life began to change on that day. My mother and my grandmother were ill and they sat on the floor, with their dogs, near the little fire.

My sister Alizon wanted to go out. 'I'm going to look for bread,' she said.

My brother James sat near the fire, his mouth open. 'Go and look for bread,' he said. 'Go and look for bread.' James often said things again and again.

Alizon ran out of the house and I followed her.

'Go and look for bread!' James called.

Alizon began to go east, up the hill and past the big trees behind Malkin Tower. Alizon walked fast. She was eighteen years old and she was tall with long, dirty brown hair and a white, hungry face. It was cold, but there was no rain. Alizon wore a coat and some shoes, but I had no coat and no shoes.

'Please wait a minute!' I called to my sister. 'I want to come with you.'

'No!' Alizon cried. 'Go back, I don't want you.'

Suddenly, a dog ran in front of Alizon.

'Good dog, good dog!' Alizon called. The dog ran to her and she put her hand on its head. It was my sister's dog and it liked her. It was a big dog with big teeth and I didn't like it because it was always hungry.

I followed Alizon and her dog along the river to Colne.

My brother James sat near the fire, his mouth open.

But before we arrived at Colne, we met John Law. John Law was a big fat man, about fifty years old.

'Can I have some money, please?' Alizon called. 'I'm hungry.'

John Law didn't answer. He walked slowly because he was fat and because he carried a big bag on his back. In his bag were a lot of beautiful things. He was a pedlar and he walked across the hills and visited all the villages.

'Can I have some money?' Alizon called again. 'I'm very hungry!'

John Law stopped. 'Stop following me,' he said. 'I'm not going to give you money.'

'Give me money!' Alizon said.

'I don't want to give you money,' the pedlar said. He took his hat off. There was not much hair on his head. 'I don't like you and I don't like your family. A lot of bad women, you are, and your father was a bad man, too.'

Alizon was angry. 'Don't talk about my father – he's dead now! Give me some money, old man!'

John Law's face was red. 'No!' he cried. He began to walk up the hill to the village. 'Go back to your dirty family!'

Alizon began to laugh angrily. 'A dead man! A dead man!' she called. 'Dead before dark, John Law!' She looked down at her dog and put her hand on its head. 'Go after him, dog,' she said. 'Go after him and get him!'

The big dog began to run after the pedlar. John Law stopped. He looked afraid and his face was very red. 'Call your dog back, you bad girl!' he shouted.

Suddenly, his mouth opened and his face went white. Slowly, he began to fall, and his big body hit the road. The dog came up to him, but the pedlar did not move.

Alizon watched John Law for a minute. Then she said to me, 'Go and call someone from the village.'

I felt afraid, but I ran along the road very quickly. 'Help! Help!' I called to the villagers. 'The pedlar is ill!'

The villagers came out of their houses and followed me down the hill. A young man looked at John Law carefully.

'He's not dead,' he said, 'but he's very ill. Let's move him to the nearest house. Someone must go and call his son.'

Just then, John Law began to talk very slowly. 'I can't move!' he said. 'I'm alive, but I can't move!'

I went back to stand near Alizon. The dog sat at her feet.

'That Device girl . . .' John Law said slowly, 'she – she cursed me! She wanted me to die! And her dog came to get me.'

All the villagers looked at Alizon.

'I'm sorry,' Alizon said quickly. 'I'm very hungry and I wanted some money, that's all.'

'Go away!' the villagers cried. 'You're a witch, and we don't want you in our village.'

Alizon began to run away down the hill and her dog

followed. I watched the villagers. They carried John Law slowly up the hill to the nearest house. And then I followed my sister down the hill. I was hungry and tired and Malkin Tower was many miles away. I was nine years old and I was angry. I was angry because the pedlar was ill. I was angry because the villagers didn't like me. And I was angry because my sister was a witch.

The villagers carried John Law slowly up the hill.

2
ROGER NOWELL

John Law was ill because Alizon cursed him, and his son wanted Roger Nowell to question Alizon. Roger Nowell was a rich and important man in Lancashire, and he was the judge for all the villages near Pendle Hill. He lived at Read Hall, seven miles from Newchurch.

On the thirtieth day of March, Mr Nowell's men came to Malkin Tower. Mr Nowell wanted to see Alizon at once.

We walked from Malkin Tower to Read Hall: my sister Alizon, my brother James, and our mother, Elizabeth Device. I followed them because I didn't want to stay at home with my grandmother. My grandmother was a difficult old woman, and I didn't like her.

Read Hall was an old house with a big garden and many old trees. Mr Nowell's servant opened the door for us.

'Come in,' Mr Nowell said. He was a tall man with a lot of white hair. His black coat looked warm and expensive.

Alizon followed Mr Nowell into a room with a big fire. When I saw the fire, I wanted to go in, too!

'Are you cold, little one?' Mr Nowell asked me. 'Come in, and sit near the fire.'

I went across the room and sat down on the floor, next to the wonderful, hot fire.

Mr Nowell sat behind a big table. Two or three men, in

black coats, stood near the window. Alizon stood in front of Mr Nowell. Her long hair was dirty, and her old dress looked dirtier.

'Two weeks ago, on the eighteenth day of March, you met John Law near Colne,' Roger Nowell said. His voice was slow and careful. 'Tell me about it.'

'I asked for money,' Alizon said. 'The pedlar was very angry and I didn't like him. I was angry, too, and I wanted him to die!'

'Tell me about your dog.'

'The dog is my friend,' Alizon said slowly. 'I wanted a friend, and I found that dog two months ago. I told my grandmother, and she liked the dog, too.'

'Did the dog run after the pedlar?'

'Yes, of course. I cursed the pedlar, and the dog ran after him!' Alizon said. 'I'm sorry now, because Mr Law is ill.'

'She's a witch!' one of the men said quietly.

Roger Nowell stood up and walked across the room to the door. 'James Device, come in. We want to question you.'

James came in and stood next to Alizon. James was thirteen years old, nearly a man, but he was afraid of many things. He began to cry.

'Don't be afraid,' Mr Nowell said. 'We want you to talk about your grandmother, Old Demdike.'

But Alizon wanted to talk. 'Don't ask him!' she said

I sat down on the floor, next to the wonderful, hot fire.

quickly. 'I can tell you about my grandmother because I'm with her every minute of the day. I go with her from village to village. I go with her across Pendle Hill. She asks people for money and food, and I help her.' Alizon stopped. She looked at James, and then she looked at Mr Nowell. 'She cursed a child once, and the child died later that year.'

'And you!' James said. 'You cursed a child, too! Somebody told me!' James suddenly sat down on the floor and began to laugh loudly.

'Be quiet!' Roger Nowell said coldly. 'Alizon Device, tell me the truth: did you curse a child?'

'Yes, I did,' Alizon cried. 'The child called me a witch, and I was angry. I cursed the child, but I was sorry when the child died.'

James looked up at Alizon, his mouth open. 'The child died, the child died,' he said again and again.

'Alizon Device, you cannot go home again,' Roger Nowell said slowly. 'You must go to the prison at Read.'

'But I need Alizon!' my mother shouted angrily from the door. 'She takes care of Old Demdike, my mother.'

I looked at my mother, at her red, angry face. I looked at Alizon in her dirty dress, and at James on the floor with his mouth open. And then I looked at Mr Nowell: his brown eyes were warm, and his face was kind.

On the second day of April, Roger Nowell and his men

The Villages of Pendle
N
W
E
S
Pendle Hill
577 metres
Malkin Tower was somewhere near here
Colne
Barley
Newchurch
Hoarstones
To Lancaster
Sabden
Sabden Brook
Ashlar House
Fence
Read
Read Hall
To London
Miles
Kilometres
Lancaster
Pendle
London

came to Ashlar House, near the village of Fence. Mr Nowell wanted to talk to my grandmother, and we all went with her to Ashlar House. Fence was not far from Malkin Tower, and my grandmother walked there easily.

Old Demdike was a little old woman with a fat face and no teeth. She was nearly eighty years old and she was a difficult old woman. Without Alizon, she was more difficult because my mother didn't take care of her.

When I saw Mr Nowell again at Ashlar House, I felt happy. I looked at his kind face and his warm brown eyes, and I wanted to be near him. But there were a lot of people in the room, and I was afraid to go to him.

'Old Demdike, I'm going to ask you some questions,' Mr Nowell began.

Old Demdike was not afraid. She looked at all the men, in their expensive coats and hats. 'What can a poor old woman tell you rich men?' She laughed, and when she laughed I felt afraid. My grandmother was going to tell them everything!

And she did!

'Twenty years ago, I met the Devil,' Old Demdike said. 'He was a boy called Tibb and he was my friend. Then a cat came to visit me – a beautiful cat – and then a dog. They were all my friends.'

Mr Nowell listened quietly to my grandmother, but some of the men began to talk angrily.

'Be careful, you rich men!' my grandmother cried. 'I can curse you! I can kill people! I make clay pictures of people – man, woman or child. And when I break the clay, that man, woman or child dies!'

People began to shout.

'She's a witch! She must die!'

'Say no more; she must die, with all her family!'

Roger Nowell stood up. 'Be quiet!' He looked at the guards near the door. 'Take her away,' he said. 'Old Demdike and her granddaughter Alizon must go to the prison at Lancaster Castle.'

'Be careful, you rich men!' Old Demdike cried.

The guards took my grandmother by the arms and carried her out of the door and put her on a horse. Everyone ran out of Ashlar House. They ran after the horses and shouted: 'Kill the witch!'

I looked for Mr Nowell, but he was on his horse, too,

Everyone ran after the horses and shouted: 'Kill the witch!'

and he followed the guards quickly through the village.

Slowly, I followed my mother and James. Malkin Tower was my home, but I didn't want to go back there. I was a little child, and I wanted someone kind to take care of me.

We stayed at home for days, because we were afraid to go out. James sat in front of the fire, with his dog, and talked. 'Lancaster Castle, Lancaster Castle,' he said, again and again. My mother hit me and shouted at me because she was angry with the rich men.

But after three days, my mother suddenly said, 'James! We're hungry and we must eat!'

James didn't answer.

My mother went across the room to James and pulled his hair. 'Get up!' she shouted. 'Go out and find food for us! Your father isn't here now; you must find food for us.' She hit him over the head.

James stood up slowly. 'Go out and find food,' he said. 'I must go out and find food.'

It was dark, and James was out for hours. But in the morning, he came back with a sheep.

'I went to Barley,' James said happily. 'I got this sheep, and now we can eat.'

'Get up, Jennet!' my mother shouted. 'Come and help me!'

It was Friday, the tenth day of April. My family had some friends, poor people, and on that day they came to Malkin Tower. They came and asked about Old Demdike and Alizon, and they stayed to eat and drink.

I helped my mother. We cooked the sheep over a big fire, and our visitors ate with us. At the same time, they drank. They sat by the fire and drank, and talked about Lancaster Castle.

'Let's go there!' an old woman cried. 'Let's go to Lancaster Castle and find Old Demdike and Alizon!'

'We can curse the guards, and break down the door!' my mother said.

'Let's bring them home!' said an old man.

'Jennet, bring the bottle! We need more drink!' shouted my mother.

I got up and took more drink to my mother. But I fell over one of the dogs, and the bottle broke on the floor. The drink was gone!

'You bad child!' my mother shouted. 'You're a witch, too, you know!' She got up and began to hit me. She hit me over the head and pulled my hair. An old man laughed, and then everyone laughed.

I ran back across the room. I wasn't a witch; I was a child, nine years old, and I hated my mother and all her friends! My face felt very hot because I was angry. I left the room and went out of the house. It was afternoon, but the

I fell over one of the dogs, and the bottle broke on the floor.

sky was dark with rain. Pendle Hill was dark, too. It sat quietly and watched me.

'I'm going to Mr Nowell,' I said quietly, to Pendle Hill. 'I'm going to tell him about my mother and her friends.'

3
A FAMILY OF WITCHES

I ran from Malkin Tower, down the hill into Newchurch. James followed me.

'I want to go to Read Hall, too,' he said.

We ran through the trees to Sabden Brook. The noise of the river was beautiful in my ears. We went along the river to the village of Sabden, and then it began to rain.

Suddenly, we heard the noise of horses behind us. We got off the road, and watched the horses. It was Roger Nowell with some of his men. They saw us, and Mr Nowell stopped.

'It's the Device children,' he said. 'What's your name, child?'

'My name is Jennet,' I said. 'We're going to Read Hall. I want to talk to you.'

Roger Nowell looked at me with his warm brown eyes. 'Very well,' he said. 'Come home with me, and we can talk.' He lifted me up on to his horse, and the horse moved

'What's your name, child?' said Mr Nowell.

quickly along the road to the village of Read. James ran along behind us.

Very soon, we arrived at Read Hall. The servant opened the door for us, and we went into the warm house.

James came in, too, and sat down next to me near the fire.

Mr Nowell put his black hat down on the table. 'Bring a hot drink and some food for these children,' he told the servant. 'They're cold and hungry.'

The servant brought bread and hot milk for us, and James and I ate hungrily. I felt warm and happy in Mr Nowell's house. I wanted to stay there all my life; I never wanted to go back to Malkin Tower.

I felt warm and happy in Mr Nowell's house.

When we finished eating, Mr Nowell looked up from his book. 'You wanted to talk to me,' he said quietly. 'Well, I'm listening.'

I got up, went across the room and stood in front of Mr Nowell. 'I'm afraid of my mother,' I began. 'I'm afraid because she's a witch and she can kill people.'

The room was quiet. Mr Nowell said nothing, but his brown eyes were kind.

'My mother and her friends are at Malkin Tower,' I told him. 'They want to go to Lancaster Castle and kill the guards. They're going to bring Old Demdike and Alizon home again.'

Mr Nowell got up and left the room. After some time, he came back with two of his friends. They all sat down at the table.

'Jennet, I want you to tell me again about your mother and her friends.'

'They want to kill the guards at Lancaster Castle and bring Old Demdike home to Malkin Tower,' I said. Then I began to cry.

'Don't cry,' Mr Nowell said kindly. 'We can help you, but we must talk to your brother first. James!' he called. 'Tell me about your mother. Is she a witch?'

'She's a witch. We're all witches,' James began. 'Old Demdike's a witch. One night, she went to the church at Newchurch and got some teeth from dead bodies there.

The Devil talked to her and she brought the teeth to Malkin Tower. They're under the ground by our door!'

'Old Demdike's a witch; we know that,' Mr Nowell said. 'Tell us about your mother.'

'Mother's a witch,' James said. 'She killed Mr Robinson, from Barley village. She made a clay picture, and then she broke it, and Mr Robinson died a week later.' James smiled at Mr Nowell. He liked Mr Nowell because Mr Nowell didn't shout at him. 'And I'm a witch, too! I can kill people!'

'Mother made a clay picture, and then she broke it, and Mr Robinson died a week later.'

'No, James!' I cried. 'You're not a witch! You don't kill people!'

'Yes, I do,' James said angrily. His face went red. 'My

dog, Dandy, is the Devil and he killed a man for me. I wanted a shirt and Mr Duckworth was going to give me one of his old shirts. But in the end, he didn't give it to me and I was very angry. I nearly killed Mr Duckworth! But I called Dandy, and he killed Mr Duckworth for me!'

I began to cry. My brother was a witch, too! All my family were witches!

'Don't cry, Jennet,' Mr Nowell said. 'Someone must take care of you. You can stay here at Read Hall with me.'

When Mr Nowell's men brought my mother to Read Hall, she said nothing at first.

'Tell us about the pictures of clay,' Mr Nowell said. 'My men found pictures of clay at Malkin Tower.'

My mother said nothing.

'Your mother, Old Demdike, is a witch. Your daughter is a witch,' Mr Nowell said. 'Your son killed Mr Duckworth because of a shirt. Now, tell us about the clay pictures.'

My mother said nothing.

'James told us about Mr Robinson of Barley,' Mr Nowell said. 'Did you kill him?'

Suddenly, my mother's face went red and she began to shout at James. 'A good son, you are! You told this rich man about Jack Robinson of Barley. Well, you told the truth. I killed him! I made a clay picture, and then I broke it, and a week later he died. I killed him because I hated him.'

She stopped and looked at me. I wanted to run away but Mr Nowell's servant stood in front of the door. Then my mother laughed. 'Jennet Device, witch's daughter! You

My mother laughed. 'Jennet Device, witch's daughter!'

hate us, I know that. Well, it doesn't matter because you're right: you *are* different. You're my daughter, but you're not the daughter of my husband. Your father was a rich man, but he never gave me money. A witch's child, he called you. And when you were born, he never came near me again. Jack Robinson learnt the truth about your father. He told the villagers of Barley and they called me a bad woman, but they didn't call your father a bad man! Nobody in Barley gave me food again, because of Jack Robinson. I hated him, and so I killed him!'

The room was very quiet and my mother laughed again.

My hands felt cold and my face was hot, but I didn't cry. When Mr Device died, I cried for days. But he was not my father. I looked at my mother, at her dirty hair and her ugly face, at her angry eyes. I hated her then, and I hated her for many years.

4
TRUTH AND LIES

On the twenty-seventh day of April, the guards took my mother and James to Lancaster Castle, and my life at Read Hall began. Suddenly, it was spring. The sky was blue and there were beautiful flowers on the hills. From Read Hall, Pendle Hill looked different: it looked smaller, and it was not so important in my life. Sometimes I walked along Sabden Brook to Sabden, and then to Newchurch, and I felt happy to be near Pendle Hill again. But I never visited Malkin Tower again.

Spring changed into summer, and in August I went to Lancaster with Mr Nowell. Lancaster was thirty miles from Read Hall, and I got very tired because I sat on a horse for hours. It was a big, noisy town. I never saw so many people before in my life and I felt afraid.

The trial of the witches of Pendle began at Lancaster Castle on the eighteenth day of August, and the judge was

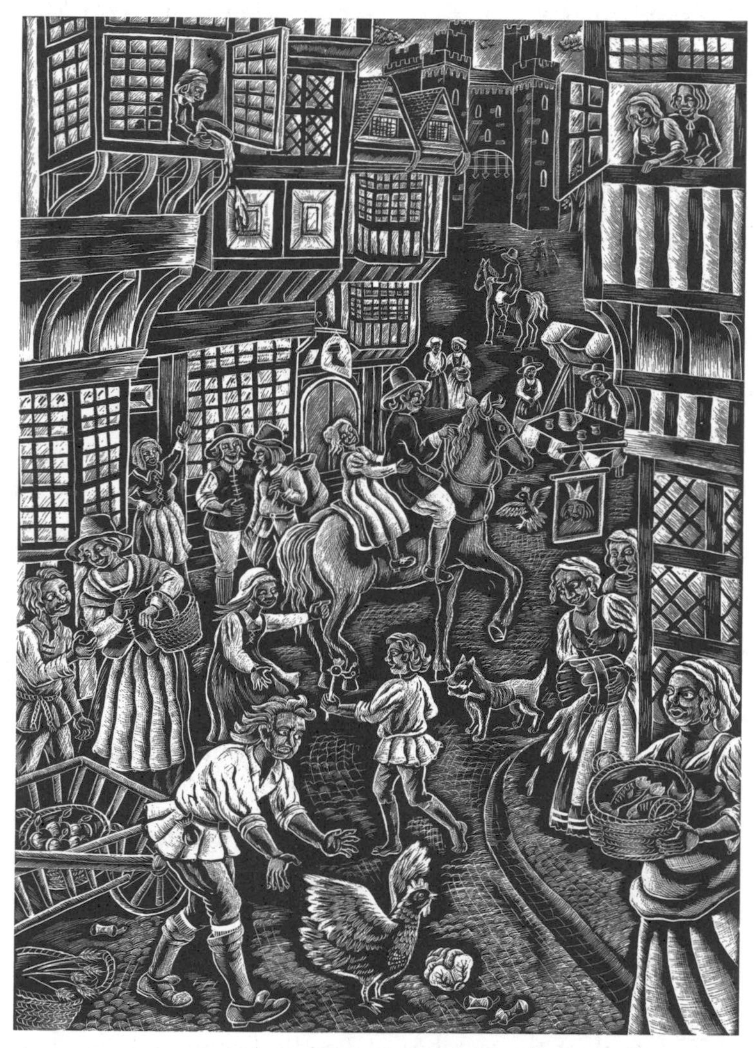

Lancaster was a big, noisy town.
I never saw so many people before in my life.

an important man from London. Judge Bromley listened to many people on that day, because there were a lot of witches from Lancashire in the prison. Old Demdike was not there because she died in May, before the judge arrived.

I waited with Mr Nowell's servant, and when a guard called my name, I went through a big door and saw the judge behind a table. Judge Bromley was rich and important, but his eyes were cold. Suddenly, I saw my mother! She was dirty and very thin. When she saw me, her face went red. My hair was clean now, and I wore shoes and an expensive dress. I saw my mother's eyes: she hated me!

'Are you a witch?' Judge Bromley asked my mother.

'No, I'm not,' my mother answered angrily.

'Did you kill Jack Robinson, of Barley village?'

'No, I did not.'

'Jennet Device is here,' a voice said quietly. It was Mr Nowell. 'She can tell us the truth about her mother.'

For a minute, my mother did not move. Then she ran across the room and shouted at me. 'You know nothing, you bad child! And I'm your mother! Don't forget that!'

The guards ran after my mother and pulled her to the floor.

'I'm no witch!' my mother shouted. 'It's all lies! Jennet, you're a witch – a child of the Devil! You're my daughter, and *I know*!'

I was afraid and I put my hands over my eyes. I didn't want to see my mother's ugly face. The guards pulled my mother out of the room and the noise stopped.

'Jennet Device,' the judge said. 'Tell us the truth about your mother.'

Roger Nowell lifted me up and put me on a table in front of the judge.

'My mother is a witch,' I began. 'She has a friend, a dog called Ball. When she wants to kill somebody, she tells Ball . . .' I talked and talked; I told the judge everything.

Judge Bromley listened carefully. 'My child, is this the truth?'

'Yes,' I answered. 'I'm telling you the truth.'

The guards brought my mother back into the room again. Her face looked tired and her eyes were red.

'Elizabeth Device, your daughter told us about your dog, Ball. Your son, too, told us about the clay pictures. We know everything.'

My mother said nothing. She didn't look at the judge and she didn't look at me.

Next, the guards brought my brother James into the room. When I saw James, I wanted to cry. James was thin and dirty and his hair was very long. He looked at the judge and at all the rich and important men in the room and he began to cry. Then he sat down on the floor.

'Stand up, James Device,' Judge Bromley said.

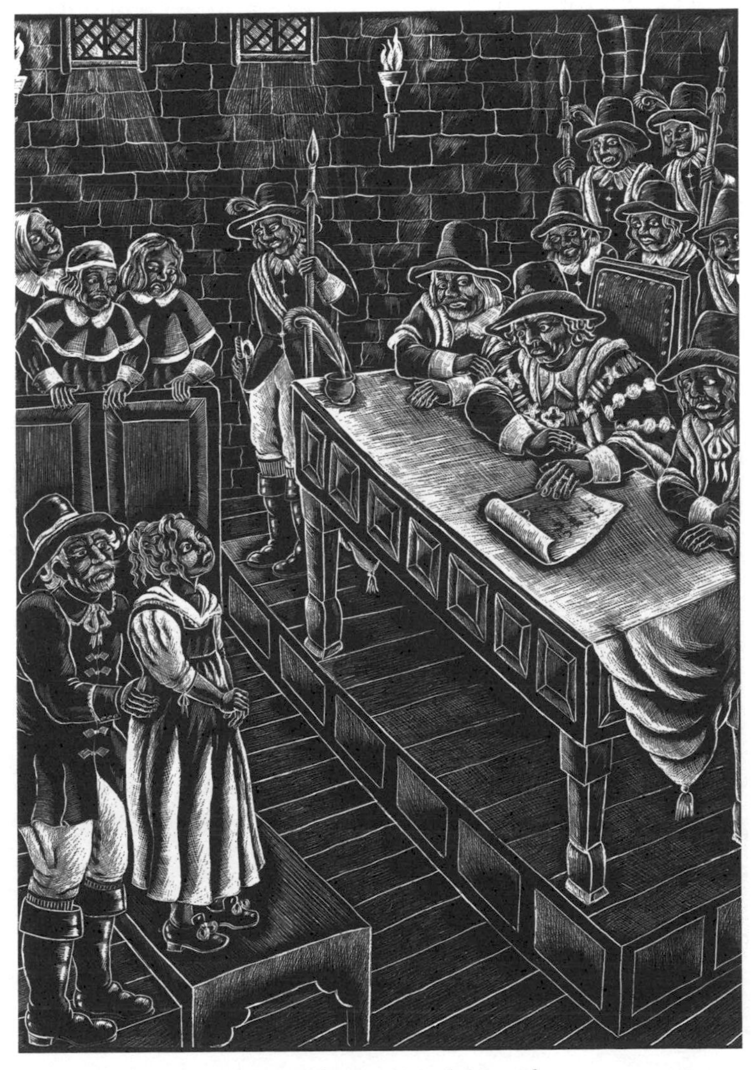

'My mother is a witch,' I said.

The guards pulled James up, but he fell to the floor again.

'You killed Mr Duckworth,' Judge Bromley said.

'I wanted a shirt,' James cried.

'Is your brother a witch?' Judge Bromley asked me.

'Yes,' I said. My brother sat on the floor, his mouth open. He looked at me, but he didn't know me. I was clean, and fat because of all the good food at Read Hall.

'James told me about his friend, Dandy,' I began. 'Dandy was the Devil and—'

The guards pulled James up, but he fell to the floor again.

James heard the name Dandy, and he began to cry again. 'I want Dandy! I want to go home!'

The guards pulled him up from the floor and took him out of the room. I never saw my brother again.

When the guards brought my sister Alizon in front of the judge, I said nothing. John Law, the pedlar, came into the room. He was a thin man now. He walked slowly and he talked slowly and his face looked ill. He told the judge about that day near Colne when Alizon cursed him and her dog ran after him.

'I'm sorry!' Alizon said. 'I was angry with you that day, but I'm sorry now.' Alizon's eyes were dark and afraid, but she had no friends in that room and nobody wanted to listen to her.

Then Mr Nowell took me out and I waited with his servant in a different room. An hour later, there was the noise of many people shouting and crying.

The servant smiled. 'The trial is finished,' he said. 'You're a good child, Jennet. You told the judge the truth about the witches.'

Mr Nowell took me home to Read Hall. And on the twentieth day of August 1612, the guards took my mother, my sister and my brother out of prison, and hanged them in front of Lancaster Castle.

They took my mother, my sister and my brother out of prison, and hanged them in front of Lancaster Castle.

And so I lost my family.

When I was a child, I wanted to be happy. I wanted to be warm, to wear shoes, to eat good food. I wanted someone to take care of me. That's all. My mother gave me nothing. She gave me no love. She never took care of me. Because my mother was a witch, my father ran away and I never knew him. My father was a rich man without a name, and I lived hungry and cold with a witch. And so I told Judge Bromley the truth about my family. Was I wrong? I don't know.

I was happy for years at Read Hall. For twenty-one years, I forgot my family. I learned to cook for the Nowell family; I worked many hours every day but I was warm and I ate good food. Every Sunday, in my best dress, I went to church; every summer I walked over Pendle Hill. I never thought about my family, because I was happy at Read Hall.

In August 1612, the guards hanged my family in front of Lancaster Castle. But their dead faces waited for me there; and a year ago, in 1633, when the guards put me in the prison in Lancaster Castle, I met them again. Day after day, I see their ugly, dead faces and hear their cold, angry voices. I think of them all the time. God is with me here, in prison. I believe that. But my dead family is with me too.

Mr Webster, from the church at Kildwick, visits me again. His blue eyes are tired, but he smiles at me.

At Read Hall I worked many hours every day but I was warm and I ate good food.

'Edmund Robinson and his father told the truth in London,' he says quietly. 'The child told lies about you because he was afraid of his father. He wanted his father to love him.'

I say nothing. Mr Webster wants to be kind, but he cannot help me. Mr Nowell cannot help me because he is dead. Edmund Robinson is only a child; he tells lies one day, and the truth the next day. But the truth cannot help me. What can I do against hate, and lies? When Mr Nowell was alive, the villagers didn't talk about me. But when Mr Nowell died, the lies began. The villagers are all afraid of me – because my name is Device. They hate me – because my name is Device. They say I am a witch – because my name is Device.

I come from a family of witches, but I am not a witch. Nobody died because I cursed them. I never made clay pictures, I never had a cat or dog. I only wanted to live quietly at Read Hall and watch the changing skies over Pendle Hill.

When I was a child, I was always cold and hungry, and I hated my family because they were witches. In 1612, I told the truth, and the truth killed my family. Now, twenty-two years later, lies are going to kill me, here in Lancaster Castle, and I am cold and hungry again.

Mr Webster gives me bread, and I go back into the prison. I can never go back to Read Hall; I know that now.

They are watching me, and waiting for me.

I must stay here in Lancaster Castle, with my dead family.

They are watching me, and waiting for me. I can never be free of them.

This is my true story; and I want to finish it now.

GLOSSARY

believe to think that something is true
castle a large, stone building
church a building where people go to pray to God
clay earth which is used to make bricks, pots, etc.
clean *(adj)* not dirty
cook *(v)* to heat food
curse *(v)* to call for bad things to happen to someone
Devil a bad spirit; the enemy of God
fall (past tense **fell**) to go down suddenly
fire something burning
floor the part of a room on which you walk
follow to come or go after someone or something
food things to eat
God the good spirit who made the world
grandmother the mother of someone's mother or father
ground what you stand or walk on
guard someone who watches a prison and stops prisoners running away
hang to kill someone by holding them above the ground with a rope around the neck
hate to dislike someone very much; opposite of 'to love'
horse a big animal that people ride on
judge *(n)* someone who decides if someone has done wrong
kind friendly and helpful
lie *(n)* something you say that is not true
life the time when someone is alive
lift *(v)* to take someone or something up

pedlar someone who walks from place to place selling small things
poor with very little money; opposite of 'rich'
prison a place where people are locked up
pull to move something nearer to you
servant someone who is paid to work in a house
sheep an animal that gives meat and wool
shout to talk very loudly
take care of to make someone happy and comfortable
thin not fat
trial when a judge and other people meet to ask questions and find out the truth about what happened
truth the things which are true
ugly not nice to look at; opposite of 'beautiful'
voice *(n)* you talk with your voice
witch a woman who can make bad things happen to people

The Witches of Pendle

ACTIVITIES

ACTIVITIES

Before Reading

1 Read the back cover and the story introduction on the first page of the book. How much do you know now about *The Witches of Pendle*? Tick one box for each sentence.

	YES	NO
1 In the 1600s many people believed in witches.	☐	☐
2 Witches were usually men.	☐	☐
3 Jennet lived near Pendle Hill.	☐	☐
4 Jennet was twelve years old in 1612.	☐	☐
5 Jennet's mother was Old Demdike.	☐	☐
6 Alizon was Jennet's sister.	☐	☐
7 In 1634 Jennet was in prison.	☐	☐

2 This story happens in England in the 1600s. What was life like then? Tick one box for each sentence.

	YES	NO
1 Every child went to school.	☐	☐
2 Many people believed in the Devil.	☐	☐
3 Poor people ate a lot of meat.	☐	☐
4 There were many doctors.	☐	☐
5 People were often ill.	☐	☐
6 Witches often cursed rich people.	☐	☐
7 Witches were usually rich.	☐	☐
8 People killed witches.	☐	☐
9 People liked witches.	☐	☐

ACTIVITIES

While Reading

Read Chapter 1, then answer these questions.

1 Where was Jennet Device in the spring of 1634?
2 Who told lies about Jennet?
3 How old was Jennet in 1634?
4 Where did Jennet and her family live in 1612?
5 What were the names of Jennet's sister and brother?
6 Why did Alison Device want money from John Law?
7 Why did Alizon curse John Law?
8 Why didn't the villagers want Alizon in their village?

Read Chapter 2. Choose the best question-word for these questions and then answer them.

Who / Why

1 . . . was Roger Nowell?
2 . . . did Jennet go with her family to Read Hall?
3 . . . told Roger Nowell all about Old Demdike?
4 . . . did Jennet's mother need Alizon at home?
5 . . . did Jennet feel happy when she saw Mr Nowell?
6 . . . were Old Demdike's friends?
7 . . . did the guards take to the prison at Lancaster Castle?
8 . . . didn't Jennet want to go home to Malkin Tower?
9 . . . did Jennet hate her mother?

Before you read Chapter 3, can you guess what happens? Choose the best ending for these sentences.

1 Jennet goes to Read Hall . . .
   a) but Mr Nowell is not there.
   b) and Mr Nowell is kind to her.
2 Jennet tells Mr Nowell about her mother . . .
   a) and he believes her.
   b) but he doesn't believe her.
3 Mr Nowell puts . . .
   a) Jennet in prison.
   b) Jennet's mother in prison.
4 After Jennet talks to Mr Nowell, . . .
   a) she stays at Read Hall and begins a new life there.
   b) she goes back home to Malkin Tower.

Read Chapter 3. Here are some untrue sentences about the chapter. Change them into true sentences.

1 The servant brought bread and hot milk for Mr Nowell.
2 Jennet wanted to stay at Malkin Tower all her life.
3 Jennet was afraid of her mother because she was a rich woman.
4 James killed Mr Duckworth because of a dog.
5 James didn't tell Mr Nowell about his mother's clay picture of Jack Robinson.
6 Mr Nowell's men found pictures of clay at Read Hall.
7 Mr Device was Jennet's father.

8 Jack Robinson didn't know the truth about Jennet's father.
9 Jennet's father always gave money to Jennet's mother.
10 Jennet loved her mother for many years.

Read Chapter 4, and then answer these questions about the trial at Lancaster Castle.

Who

1 . . . had clean hair, wore shoes and an expensive dress?
2 . . . called Jennet 'a child of the Devil'?
3 . . . said, 'I'm telling you the truth'?
4 . . . sat on the floor, with his mouth open?
5 . . . was thin and ill, and walked and talked slowly?
6 . . . was sorry about the pedlar?
7 . . . died on 20 August 1612 in front of Lancaster Castle?

Now choose the best words to finish Jennet's story.

Before / After the trial, Jennet lived happily at *Read Hall / Malkin Tower* for many years. She wanted to *remember / forget* her family, but when Roger Nowell died, the villagers began to tell *lies / the truth* about her. They hated her *so / because* she came from a family of witches. Jennet *was / was not* a witch, but in 1633 she went *to prison / home* – because her name was Device. Her family was *dead / alive*, but Jennet could *always / never* be free of them.

After Reading

1 Use this table to make true sentences about the people in this story. (You can use the words more than once.)

Roger Nowell				Alizon Device
John Law				his father
Elizabeth Device				her mother
Alizon Device		angry	to	the rich men
Edmund Robinson	was	afraid	with	John Law
Mr Webster	wasn't	kind	about	Jennet Device
Jennet Device		sorry	of	Mr Duckworth
James Device				the judge
Old Demdike				her daughter

2 Do you agree (A) or disagree (D) with these sentences? Explain why.

1 The Devices killed many people.

2 There were witches in the 1600s, but there are no witches now.

3 The Devices were poor and hungry, but they were not witches.

4 The Devices were not witches, but they were bad people.

5 Jennet told the truth about her family.

3 Choose the right words and endings from the list below to complete these sentences about Jennet and her family.

JENNET was the youngest _____. Her father was a rich man, _________. Years later, Jennet went to prison _________.
ELIZABETH DEVICE was Jennet's _____. She hated Jack Robinson _________. The villagers called her a bad woman, _________.
OLD DEMDIKE was Jennet's _____. She made clay pictures of people _________. The guards took her to the prison at Lancaster Castle, _________.
ALIZON DEVICE was Jennet's _____. She cursed a child _________. But she was sorry _________.
JAMES DEVICE was Jennet's _____. He asked Mr Duckworth for a shirt, ________. So James called his dog, ________.

brother / child / grandmother / mother / sister

1 but she died before the trial in August.
2 but Mr Duckworth didn't give it to him.
3 because he told the villagers about Jennet's father.
4 because the child called her a witch.
5 because Edmund Robinson told lies about her.
6 but they didn't call Jennet's father a bad man.
7 and the dog killed Mr Duckworth.
8 when the child died.
9 but she lived cold and hungry with a family of witches.
10 and when she broke them, the people died.

4 Here is a conversation between Roger Nowell and John Law's son, Mr Law (see page 11). The conversation is in the wrong order. Write it out in the correct order and put in the speakers' names. Mr Law speaks first (number 7).

1 _____ 'I know him. He often visits Read Hall. Why do you want to talk to me about him?'

2 _____ 'The Device family is very poor, I know. So, what happened?'

3 _____ 'Who is your father?'

4 _____ 'No, he's not dead, but he's very ill. He can talk but he can't move.'

5 _____ 'Because a witch cursed him yesterday.'

6 _____ 'I don't know. She ran away with her sister and the dog.'

7 _____ 'Mr Nowell, can I talk to you about my father?'

8 _____ 'Is he dead?'

9 _____ 'My father is John Law, the pedlar.'

10 _____ 'The Device girls and their dog followed my father to Colne. They wanted money.'

11 _____ 'Well, they live at Malkin Tower, I know. My men can find them and bring them to Read Hall.'

12 _____ 'Mmm, that's bad. I must talk to the Device girl. Where is she now?'

13 _____ 'One of the girls cursed my father. Then her dog ran after him, and at once he fell on to the road.'

14 _____ 'A witch? What happened? Tell me about it.'

5 **Before he died, perhaps Mr Nowell wrote a letter to Mr Webster. Use these words from the story to complete the letter. (Use each word once.)**

afraid, because, brother, care, church, cooks, dead, hanged, happy, hates, hungry, kind, prison, remember, so, trial, truth, when, witch

Dear Mr Webster

I am leaving this letter _____ I am going to die soon and you can help Jennet. She came to Read Hall in 1612 _____ she was nine years old. I wanted to take _____ of Jennet because she was a poor, _____ child and she was _____ of her family. Old Demdike, the grandmother, was a _____. She died in _____. Her mother, her sister and her _____ were witches, too. At the _____ Jennet told the _____ to Judge Bromley, and the guards _____ her family.

Jennet lives here at Read Hall and _____ for my family. She is _____ here, I know. She goes to _____ every Sunday and she is a good woman. She _____ the Devil and she is not a witch. But the villagers _____ Old Demdike and the Device witches. Jennet is a Device and _____ the villagers are afraid of her. When I am _____, please be _____ to Jennet and take care of her. Thank you!

Your friend,

Roger Nowell

ABOUT THE AUTHOR

Rowena Akinyemi is British, and after many years in Africa, she now lives and works in Cambridge. She has worked in English Language Teaching for twenty years, in Africa and England, and has been writing ELT fiction for ten years. She has written several other stories for the Oxford Bookworms Library, including *Remember Miranda* and *Under the Moon* (both at Stage 1). She has also written books for children.

Her family lived near Pendle Hill for ten years, and before she wrote this story, she read many history books about witches in seventeeth-century England and about the Device family. All the people in *The Witches of Pendle* were real people who lived in the seventeenth century. Malkin Tower has gone, but all the other places and villages are still there in Lancashire today. A well-known novel, *Mist over Pendle* (1951) by Robert Neill, tells an exciting story about the witches of Pendle.

OXFORD BOOKWORMS LIBRARY

Classics • Crime & Mystery • Factfiles • Fantasy & Horror
Human Interest • Playscripts • Thriller & Adventure
True Stories • World Stories

The OXFORD BOOKWORMS LIBRARY provides enjoyable reading in English, with a wide range of classic and modern fiction, non-fiction, and plays. It includes original and adapted texts in seven carefully graded language stages, which take learners from beginner to advanced level. An overview is given on the next pages.

All Stage 1 titles are available as audio recordings, as well as over eighty other titles from Starter to Stage 6. All Starters and many titles at Stages 1 to 4 are specially recommended for younger learners. Every Bookworm is illustrated, and Starters and Factfiles have full-colour illustrations.

The OXFORD BOOKWORMS LIBRARY also offers extensive support. Each book contains an introduction to the story, notes about the author, a glossary, and activities. Additional resources include tests and worksheets, and answers for these and for the activities in the books. There is advice on running a class library, using audio recordings, and the many ways of using Oxford Bookworms in reading programmes. Resource materials are available on the website <www.oup.com/elt/gradedreaders>.

The *Oxford Bookworms Collection* is a series for advanced learners. It consists of volumes of short stories by well-known authors, both classic and modern. Texts are not abridged or adapted in any way, but carefully selected to be accessible to the advanced student.

You can find details and a full list of titles in the *Oxford Bookworms Library Catalogue* and *Oxford English Language Teaching Catalogues*, and on the website <www.oup.com/elt/gradedreaders>.

THE OXFORD BOOKWORMS LIBRARY GRADING AND SAMPLE EXTRACTS

STARTER • 250 HEADWORDS

present simple – present continuous – imperative –
can/cannot, must – *going to* (future) – simple gerunds …

Her phone is ringing – but where is it?

Sally gets out of bed and looks in her bag. No phone. She looks under the bed. No phone. Then she looks behind the door. There is her phone. Sally picks up her phone and answers it. ***Sally's Phone***

STAGE 1 • 400 HEADWORDS

… past simple – coordination with *and*, *but*, *or* –
subordination with *before*, *after*, *when*, *because*, *so* …

I knew him in Persia. He was a famous builder and I worked with him there. For a time I was his friend, but not for long. When he came to Paris, I came after him – I wanted to watch him. He was a very clever, very dangerous man. ***The Phantom of the Opera***

STAGE 2 • 700 HEADWORDS

… present perfect – *will* (future) – *(don't) have to, must not, could* –
comparison of adjectives – simple *if* clauses – past continuous –
tag questions – *ask/tell* + infinitive …

While I was writing these words in my diary, I decided what to do. I must try to escape. I shall try to get down the wall outside. The window is high above the ground, but I have to try. I shall take some of the gold with me – if I escape, perhaps it will be helpful later. ***Dracula***

STAGE 3 • 1000 HEADWORDS

... *should, may* – present perfect continuous – *used to* – past perfect – causative – relative clauses – indirect statements ...

Of course, it was most important that no one should see Colin, Mary, or Dickon entering the secret garden. So Colin gave orders to the gardeners that they must all keep away from that part of the garden in future. ***The Secret Garden***

STAGE 4 • 1400 HEADWORDS

... past perfect continuous – passive (simple forms) – *would* conditional clauses – indirect questions – relatives with *where/when* – gerunds after prepositions/phrases ...

I was glad. Now Hyde could not show his face to the world again. If he did, every honest man in London would be proud to report him to the police. ***Dr Jekyll and Mr Hyde***

STAGE 5 • 1800 HEADWORDS

... future continuous – future perfect – passive (modals, continuous forms) – *would have* conditional clauses – modals + perfect infinitive ...

If he had spoken Estella's name, I would have hit him. I was so angry with him, and so depressed about my future, that I could not eat the breakfast. Instead I went straight to the old house. ***Great Expectations***

STAGE 6 • 2500 HEADWORDS

... passive (infinitives, gerunds) – advanced modal meanings – clauses of concession, condition

When I stepped up to the piano, I was confident. It was as if I knew that the prodigy side of me really did exist. And when I started to play, I was so caught up in how lovely I looked that I didn't worry how I would sound. ***The Joy Luck Club***

BOOKWORMS · TRUE STORIES · STAGE 1

Ned Kelly: A True Story

CHRISTINE LINDOP

When he was a boy, he was poor and hungry. When he was a young man, he was still poor and still hungry. He learnt how to steal horses, he learnt how to fight, he learnt how to live – outside the law. Australia in the 1870s was a hard, wild place. Rich people had land, poor people didn't. So the rich got richer, and the poor stayed poor.

Some say Ned Kelly was a bad man. Some say he was a good man but the law was bad. This is the true story of Australia's most famous outlaw.

BOOKWORMS · CLASSICS · STAGE 1

The Withered Arm

THOMAS HARDY

Retold by Jennifer Bassett

A woman and a man . . . words of love whispered on a summer night. Later, there is a child, but no wedding-ring. And then the man leaves the first woman, finds a younger woman, marries her . . . It's an old story.

Yes, it's an old, old story. It happens all the time – today, tomorrow, a hundred years ago. People don't change. But this story, set among the green hills of southern England, has something different about it. Perhaps it is only a dream, or perhaps it is magic – a kind of strange dark magic that begins in the world of dreams and phantoms . . .